THE PURPOSE
—*of*—
BEING
HIDDEN
PREPARING TO PROSPER

RHODA BANKS, LCSW

The Purpose of Being Hidden
Copyright © 2011 by Rhoda Banks

ACKNOWLEDGMENTS

I would like to give thanks to my Lord and Savior, Jesus Christ, who made this project possible by giving me divine revelation, as well as providing me with the right materials to bring this book to life.

I would also like to thank my father, Bennett Gordon, who always supports and encourages me to continue writing to the glory of God. Thanks for all your marketing efforts.

Thanks to Pastor Phil and Caroline Gauthier, for your constant encouragement and support to keep spreading the Word of God in both spoken and written form.

Thanks to Kathy Lombardo, who keeps me moving forward toward the goal and encouraging me along the way.

ENDORSEMENTS

"What great revelation Rhoda shares with us in her excellent book, *The Purpose of Being Hidden*. Not only does it give meaning to our seasons of 'hiddenness,' but it becomes a map for your personal journey. Amazing truths that are nuggets of gold are laying right before you as you pick this book up and digest it! You will be helped in the mysteries and purposes in that 'hidden place.' You will not be disappointed, no matter where you are in your journey, with the truths Rhoda has unfolded for you. Read it, share it, and discover it! *The Purpose of Being Hidden!*"

Dr. Brian Simmons
Founder, Apostolic Resource Center, West Haven, CT

"To be an effective vessel that God can work through, one must understand how He prepares us for His service. This is particularly true regarding how God fashions leaders. In her book entitled, *The Purpose of Being Hidden*, Rhoda Banks shares how God develops His servant leaders (and all believers of Christ Jesus) into men and women of purity and enduring resolve. He does this by teaching them to overcome obscurity, rejection, and even misunderstanding. I believe that this book will serve as an encouragement and strength for the reader. May you be blessed as you become all that God has called you to be."

Dr. Phil Gauthier
Senior/Founding Pastor, Hope in Life Church, Carmel, NY

CONTENTS

The Making of a Leader

The process of developing godly character often extends into a span of many years. God hides His leaders to prepare them so they will be ready to step into all that He has planned even before the foundation of the world. God has good works prepared for us. Even Jesus did not enter into His ministry until He was thirty years old. He learned how to submit to His earthly parents. The Bible states He "increased in wisdom and stature and in favor with God and man" (Luke 2:52). He stayed faithful to wait to be revealed until the appointed time.

Joseph likewise had to wait thirteen years before entering into his ministry. Although he experienced setbacks and trials, the Lord lifted him up, once he gave up his plans and dreams. When all looked lost, God sent Pharaoh a dream and the cupbearer remembered Joseph's ability to interpret dreams. This became a starting point for God to begin to prepare Joseph for his prison release. You may feel that you have been forgotten, but you are just now starting.

Although there is a call on a person's life, God allows one to be stretched and molded. This involves the refining fire, which burns away the dross. Being hidden helps one to remain humble and rely solely on the Lord. Without being hidden, we are still in the flesh, working our own agenda.

Spending time with God in the hidden place will birth His kingdom initiatives within our lives. Birthing involves contractions, but as we stay positioned and ready we are able to partake of His divine promises. We must keep the fire stirred up, and press through into conception. Consecration to His ways is essential at this stage, for it will allow His plans to come to fruition. Before we are able to handle more authority, we have to be pruned and refined. This enables us to be transformed so we have the mind of Christ. If we are not pruned, we remain immature and unable to handle higher levels of God's power and authority. Greater levels of leadership require greater consecration. Pastor Phil Gauthier mentioned to me that being hidden by God can actually become a welcome place, as in it one can find renewing of relationship with the Lord. God is jealous and wants us to want Him above everything else, including a fruitful ministry.

THE FUTURE IS GREAT

Praying in the Spirit allows us to keep our faith intact through times of trial. We need to "prime the pump" continuously so we can stay encouraged. We will be brought out into the open when God is ready to release us into our destiny. We have to remain convinced that He wants the best for us, and that He is planning a great future for us. God has good gifts stored up for His children. He wants us to live with an expectancy of hope. He will supply what we need in His time. We know God is waiting in anticipation, for He desires to bless us more than what we can think or ask. We know His desire is for our good, because He has our best interest at heart.

The Purpose of Being Hidden

Fifteen years ago I was looking for a car at a nearby dealership. As I surveyed the car lot, I spotted a shiny, two door, red Blazer that beckoned to me. I went into the shop and inquired about it. They said that the red Blazer was not the one on sale, they had another. The door of the garage flew open to reveal a two tone, four door red Blazer. Wow, what a deal! This one had style and it was even better than the first. It was hidden in the garage, where they were washing it off. I knew this vehicle was for me. I bought it and the salesman drove it back on the lot. Immediately after this, a man saw the car and began yelling, "I love that car, it has my company's colors." I told him it was already sold. God was hiding the car for me. What a thought! God hides the best for the fullness of time. "But, on the contrary, as the Scripture says, What eye has not seen and ear has not heard and has not entered into the heart of man, [all that] God has prepared [Made and keeps ready] for those who love Him [who hold Him in affectionate reverence, promptly obeying Him and gratefully recognizing the benefits He has bestowed]" (I Corinthians 2:9, AMP).

FOSTERING DEPENDENCY ON GOD

When God chooses a leader He must break him of his surroundings, and bring him to an unfamiliar place where he is forced to rely on God. Many of the patriarchs had to go to places where they were forced to start over. It allowed them to grow in their dependency on God, and not to cling to the familiar. Likewise, Abraham had to leave his homeland to inherit the blessing. He had to leave his family and friends and walk in faith.

God wants to break old associations, which lead to sin. He is breaking up the fallow ground that does not bear fruit. In due season, you will reap if you don't lose heart.

Being a godly leader takes fortitude, courage and a willingness to go at it alone when necessary. He wants you to take comfort in the fact that you are being led. Jesus is guiding you with His eyes upon you. He will bring you out of a place of restriction, as you take the Lord's words seriously and stop living just to get by. There is destiny in all of us.

God wants His people to believe Him despite setbacks, or disappointments. He will give you what you need, as you leave behind the things that stop the flow of God. He has not forgotten about you, Jesus has you on His mind! He knows your thoughts and He is intimately involved in your life. So, we have to understand that God wants you to trust Him even when things don't make sense. He is working behind the scenes to see you prosper. "For I know the thoughts that I think toward you, says the Lord, thoughts of peace and not of evil, to give you a future and a hope" (Jeremiah 29:11).

There is an established time for everything under the sun. Like the sons of Issachar, we must ask for an ability to discern the times and seasons (1 Chronicles 12:32). What God does in one season, He may not do in another. The Lord desires to bring us into a place where we will be encouraged and made whole. He will recompense us for what we have gone through in previous seasons, but we have to believe that He is a God who is faithful and true. God keeps His promises and works diligently to see His plans come to pass. He will finish what He has started. There is an order in the kingdom and He wants us to be convinced that we are being brought to a place of restoration and divine structure.

PROVING AND PASSING

Leaders must always come into a place where they submit to authority before they can aspire to advance. There is a proving and testing season that takes place before a leader can be put into position. As the leader gives over his control of his life, he finds that there will be a day of fulfillment on what God has promised. It's not what you can do to please others, but what God will do through you as you yield your vessel to His headship. It's time to remain in His love, as you prepare to enter into all that He has purposed for you. Stay encouraged, for you will see many good days and you will be taken to a place of fulfillment, as you live to honor God in all your ways.

The Bible appears to point out three different backgrounds that leaders go through. The first is a childhood (like Jesus), that does not give much detail or is nondescript. The second one is where the person has destiny, but many reversals of fortune occur before they are lifted up. Biblical examples of this can be seen in the lives of Joseph, Moses, and David. The third type is where a person trains under a mentor, and the baton gets passed on. This happened with Elijah and Elisha, also with Moses and Joshua. We too are heirs of the King. Jesus chose us before the foundation of the world to rule and reign with Him.

Here is what Bill Johnson has to say about Jesus passing the baton to believers: "Jesus came as the light of the world. He then passed the baton to us announcing that we are the light of the world. Jesus came as the Miracle Worker. He said that we would do 'greater works' than He did (John 14:12). He then pulled the greatest surprise of all, saying, 'right now the Holy Spirit is with you, but He's going to be in you.' Jesus, who illustrates to us what is possible for those who are *right with God*, now says that His people are to be the tabernacle of God on planet earth. Paul affirms this revelation with statements such as 'Do you not know that you are the temple of God?'(1 Corinthians 3:16) and 'you are a dwelling place of God.' (Ephesians 2:22)." [1]

---

1. Bill Johnson, When Heaven Invades Earth, Shippensburg, PA, Destiny Image Publishers, 2003.

Rhoda Banks

As we take God's words seriously, we are able to do "the greater works." As we allow Him to have His way in our lives; we are able to enjoy the fruits of righteousness. When we allow His winnowing fork to separate the profane from the divine, we emerge stronger and more resilient because the Holy Spirit has been given preeminence over the old nature. Becoming a leader will entail being broken and poured out, and a desert experience will often follow. Being hidden helps us stay connected to the vine, so we can gain nourishment from Him, as we learn to submit to our Savior's timing and instruction.

Godly character is forged in the valley of Achor (trouble), but God is a God of restoration. As the Bible says in Hosea 2:15, he is able to make the valley of Achor to be a door of hope. Hosea is a picture of God's faithfulness to the covenant promises, even when Israel was unfaithful. Likewise, Jesus bought us back by His blood, even when we were sinners.

Ephesians 2:10 states that for we are God's [own] handiwork [His workmanship], recreated in Christ Jesus, [born anew] that we may do those good works which God predestined [planned beforehand] for us [taking paths which he prepared ahead of time], that we should walk in them [living the good life which he prearranged and made ready for us to live] (AMP).

We are God's ambassadors here on the earth. He wants us to correctly represent Him, so He can be seen through our lives. We must be purified so we can share in His glory. And as we live to please Jesus, we are bringing the kingdom down on earth and making it visible.

The Wilderness Experience

An essential part of being hidden is passing through the wilderness test. The Wilderness is a "proving ground." This is where faith is tested and all the impurities become evident and come to the surface. Testing always proves the quality and strength of a substance. It shows where a weaknesses lies, and where adjustments need to be made. It brings our fears and doubts into play. This intense time causes us to question who we are, and what God is doing in our lives. Prior to moving into our destiny, God must test our motives to see if we will choose Him above all else.

Death to Self

Many times there is a choice to be made. God asked Abraham to sacrifice his only son. This was the son he waited many years for, the son God promised him. But God wanted to prove Abraham's faith. The testing time refines our faith and helps us to rely on God, and not our own strength or abilities. If we fail during this time, our destiny can be aborted. "but God *is* faithful, who will not allow you to be tempted beyond what you are able, but with the temptation/ trial will also make the way of escape, that you may be able to bear *it*" (1 Corinthians 10:13). As with Abraham, He provided a substitute in the thicket.

This relinquishment on Abraham's part really demonstrated that he had indeed died to himself. Dying to self is a major part of inheriting the promises. The flesh needs to be crucified, so the promises of God can come to pass. For example, Moses experienced much rejection and isolation in the wilderness. There he learned how to raise sheep for his father-in-law. His hopes for the future were dashed, and he became a servant. The dying of self caused him to look to God for his sustenance, rather than the fleeting pleasures of Egypt. The wilderness removed all pride, ambition and self-effort. What is within your life will be discovered in the wilderness.

The wilderness brings us to the end of ourselves, and our ways of doing things our way. When we are in a place of solitude and nothing seems to be working, we look up and listen for God's voice. This preparation gives us authority to be able to speak for God, in a way that can't be gleaned any other way.

Likewise Moses' time of preparation was over when God spoke to him through the burning bush. His mission was made clear; to deliver the Israelites. This was Moses' defining moment. The burning bush represents the fire of God. Fire often signifies refining, which comes with the call of God on a person's life. There must be a consecration to the will and purposes of God in all our lives.

Moses recognized the call of God on his life as a youngster, but he knew he must keep his Hebrew heritage a secret, until he could come of age where he could take care of himself. Moses chose to suffer with his people rather than enjoy the pleasures of sin. He felt that if others knew who he was; they would kill him on the spot. But Moses waited until later; when he rebelled against the way he grew up. The Egyptians cursed him but God restored his favor as a result of his fall.

The Purpose of Being Hidden

REJECTION AND THE FEAR OF MAN

One of the hallmarks of the wilderness experience is the pain of rejection. It comes in many forms, but it teaches us to cleave to God, and not people. Man is often fickle, and God tells us the fear of man is a snare. To be an effective leader, one must honor God first and not be preoccupied with what others think. If we honor God, he will honor us. To reach our destiny we must move out of our comfort zone. In order to do this, we must be healed of the fear of man. We seek to keep ourselves in the love of God, while trusting Him to move on our behalf. We must continue to seek His face, for as we do, we will find Him. It's not what we can do for God, it's what He will do through a yielded vessel who has counted the cost.

In Judges 11, we see Jephtahah, a mighty warrior who endured rejection. His background left something to be desired, (he was the son of a harlot), but he knew God. His father was Gilead. Judges 11:2-3 states, "Gilead's wife bore sons; and when his wife's sons grew up, they drove Jephthah out, and said to him, 'You shall have no inheritance in our father's house, for you *are* the son of another woman.' Then Jephthah fled from his brothers and dwelt in the land of Tob." However, when the Ammonites declared war against Israel, the elders of Gilead, wanted him to lead them in battle. Judges 11:7 states, "So Jephthah said to the elders of Gilead, 'Did you not hate me, and expel me from my father's house? Why have you come to me now when you are in distress?'"

Jephthah knew they were taking advantage of him, but he trusted the Lord to settle the account. If the Lord gave the Ammonites into his hand, he would lead the army. Although Jephthah could have nursed his wounds, he believed God's call on his life, despite his upbringing. It appears that his father was absent, and he probably never knew his mother. However we see that our gifts will make room for us. God elevates us by using the talents and abilities He gives for His glory.

MAKE ROOM FOR FORGIVENESS

God delights in turning impossible situations into possible ones. We must learn to keep short accounts, so we can move into what God has preordained for us. If we hold onto our privilege to be right, we can forfeit our destiny. God is not mocked, what we have sown, we shall reap. In other words, if we harbor bitter roots, we will reap what we said we would never become. An inner vow results from that judgment.

For example, if we harbor a grudge against our parents, and say we will never be like them, we bring a curse against ourselves, it's a judgment that will eventually cause us to have troubles in the same areas. To break free, we must forgive and take our problems to the cross. We must pray for those who mistreat us. At times we may also need deliverance.

Matthew 7:1-3 explains; "Judge not, that you be not judged. For with what judgment you judge, you will be judged; and with the measure you use, it will be measured back to you. And why do you look at the speck in your brother's eye, but do not consider the plank in your own eye?"

We have to live in such a way as to command respect from those whose viewpoints differ from ours. We have to give others the benefit of the doubt, and not allow the enemy to cause division in relationships. If we stay filled up with the Spirit, we can avert having the enemy of our soul whisper misgivings about those we love. If we are to prosper, we must take our concerns to the Lord, and allow Him to give us His perspective on our problems. For as we allow Him to be our Redeemer, we give up our right to hold onto anything that would hinder our relationship with the Lover of our soul. It's imperative to honor people, but as we acknowledge their failings, we know that we too have our issues. But we must train ourselves in right living, so we can stand in the evil days ahead. As we grow in grace, we learn to believe the best about others, and we allow God to have His way in our lives. This means we don't talk about others behind their backs, and we learn to confront honestly about our misgivings. As we nurture relationships in our lives, we begin to take back what the enemy has stolen. We are encouraged that the Lord is working to see relationships reconciled.

There are occasions, where we are not able to work out issues. We need to bring them to God, and leave the problem there. By rehashing old issues, we are walking as mere men. As we develop a mindset that leaves all vengeance with God, we are able to walk in His freedom and be unencumbered by situations. When we keep ourselves in the love of God, we are able to break through areas of resistance that were previously impenetrable. When we allow others room to make mistakes, and to even leave us (by death, desertion, or disaster), we are enabled to enter into a more intimate relationship with the Lord. Letting others be free allows us more freedom

Remember in the year King Uzziah died (in a vision) Isaiah saw the Lord, sitting upon His throne high and lifted up (Isaiah 6:1). His ministry started that year. Sometimes a death must occur to see the Lord clearly. When we become dependent upon other things instead of the Lord, we can become distracted.

Psalm 27:10 says, "although my father and my mother have forsaken me, yet the Lord will take me up [adopt me as His child] (AMP). It's not what others say about you that counts, but who God says you are. You are His special treasure, the apple of His eye. He will recompense you in due time for the injuries inflicted by others. He is able to turn things around and bring healing. For it's His good purpose to bring you out of the pit and into the palace. Remember what God did for Joseph, He will do for you. The "Joseph Company" is rising out of obscurity into places of prominence. God wants you to be part of the "Joseph Company."

Are you going through a time of rejection now? Take heart, your Heavenly Father knows your heartache and He will bring you His comfort and peace. You are being prepared for a greater destiny. God is using His pruning shears to remove what will be harmful in the long run. As you allow Jesus to take your walk to a new level, He will bring you new delights along the way. It is His good pleasure to see you take your rightful place in the kingdom.

ALL THINGS WORK TOGETHER

One of the major benefits of going through the wilderness is that we begin to see how God is working all things together for His good purpose (Romans 8:28). We begin to hear His voice clearly, and we learn how to distinguish His voice from the other voices in our lives. This enables us to experience God's grace and to know Him intimately. We allow the Lord's voice to lead us over our feelings. This helps us to cope with everything we are going through. When we cleave to God and trust that He will fulfill His good purpose for us, we gain momentum.

Being hidden is a time when everything seems to be going in the wrong direction. Because of this, it is imperative to have prophetic vision, to hang on to the promises we have been given, and to decree them over our lives. We must contend for the faith. We are gaining ground for the kingdom when we fight the good fight of faith, and stop going by what we see in the natural. The wilderness is the training ground for leaders. To endure it, we must be mindful of the fact that God will not forget your work and labors of love. The enemy desires that you stop doing what God has called you to do. The devil wants you to slack off and become apathetic. In this way satan can stop you from gaining ground for the kingdom. He wants you to live a joyless life, where life can wear you down.

But we must recognize the enemy's devices and speak to the mountains, telling them to come down. We must not hesitate to decree into existence the things that are not seen and call them as they are.

We must keep our armor on at all times, and learn to speak God's Word into our circumstance. This is because God's Word is His will. It does not return void. The waiting period is intended to help us develop strong spiritual muscles, so when the winds of adversity blow, we are like the strong Redwood trees. We are under girded with the Word of God and with prayer. We gain strength when we go to our Source, and allow Him to feed us spiritual manna that will help us to grow and develop. We grow anemic as a result of inadequate feedings of the Word. There is an increasing strength when we pray, praise, and proclaim the truth.

A TIME TO PREPARE

When we realize that the wilderness is often a preparation time prior to being revealed, we can be assured that whatever we left—or died to—was necessary for God to remove. As we allow His pruning shears to cut out what hinders our walk, we are able to bring God great glory. Oftentimes, we must learn to forgive those who have hurt us during this time. When we become better, not bitter, we are able to comfort those who are going through similar situations.

Likewise, before Jesus entered into ministry, He was sent into the wilderness by the Holy Spirit. He confronted the devil by speaking God's Word and not allowing satan to gain a foothold. He did not compromise under pressure.

Rhoda Banks

He was at a low point, where He was tempted, but did not give in. At each point the devil tried to get Jesus to abort His ministry and purpose. He even tried to tell Jesus to kill Himself by jumping down from a gable in the temple. The devil aimed the darts at Jesus' identity by saying, "If You are the Son of God, throw Yourself down from here" (Luke 4:9).

It can be seen that prior to entering into the purposes of God, there is a lot of warfare. Many times the breakthrough is right around the corner. However, during this time, the devil tries to discourage the promises that the Lord has spoken to you. He will cause you to question your calling and say you are disqualified. His primary weapon is deception, through the use of lies. Many times, before the call of God on your life is realized, there will be an attack on your character. We must press through the narrow opening until we give birth. The joy of fulfillment will be worth the pain. The dream looks hopeless, all the while; your territory is being enlarged.

I waited ten years before becoming a Christian counselor. It looked hopeless, but one day when I worked in New Rochelle, New York, the Lord told me that His delays were not denials. Shortly after that, I was transferred to Rockland Psychiatric Center. Although this was farther from home, I was able to attend Alliance Theological Seminary at night, which was in nearby Nyack.

I took the Person in Ministry course. It talked about the preparation needed to enter the ministry and pitfalls to avoid. During this time, I remember that we formed small groups, and everyone said what their ministry would be. I wondered if I would ever become a Christian counselor. But little did I know that after the second course, which was only a few months away, I would begin my private practice.

Likewise when the devil stopped his temptations, Luke 4:14 says that "Jesus went back full of and under the power of the [Holy] Spirit into Galilee, and the fame of Him spread through the whole region round about" (AMP). In other words, He was prepared for ministry and after the test, His ministry was expanded. After testing comes promotion. We must remain steadfast while waiting and not lose heart. God is working on our behalf. He is not unjust to forget our labor and He will fulfill what He has started.

STAYING STEADFAST

We need to remember that God wants us to keep our faith under fire. He wants us to stay focused on what He is doing in our lives and not what the enemy is trying to do. The enemy has already been defeated. We need to remain thankful and praise God through it all. We need to raise our expectations that what God has promised He will do. "Now to Him Who, by (in consequence of) the [action of His] power that is at work within us, is able to [carry out His purpose and] do superabundantly, far over and above all that we [dare] ask or think [infinitely beyond our highest prayers, desires, thoughts, hopes, or dreams]" (Ephesians 3:20, AMP).

Today, many people are going through a financial wilderness with unemployment or decreased wages. As times get more desperate, many will fall below the poverty line. A persevering spirit is needed. Divine strategy and direction is required. We need to get a hold of God's will for our lives and maintain an attitude of hope. For God has not forgotten about you. He has a plan for good to bring you into the Promised Land. But we must remain steadfast and immovable so we can inherit the promises.

By faith and patience the promises were inherited. (Hebrews: 6:12). We need to preserve to see the final outcome of our faith. James 1:3-4 drives the point home saying, "be assured

21

and understand that the trial and proving of your faith bring out endurance, steadfastness, and patience. But let endurance, steadfastness, and patience have full play and do a thorough work, so that you may be [people] perfectly and fully developed [with no defects], lacking in nothing" (AMP). God allows the waiting period to develop the fruits of the Spirit in us. He is building a highway of holiness that enables us to participate in His divine nature.

We must keep coming to the throne of grace to find help in time of need. This enables us to stand firm and to keep our faith intact in trying times. As we continue to speak to the mountains of doubt and to decree that we have favor, we are enabled to remain unmoved and confident that He is working on our behalf. For as we acknowledge our utter dependence on God, we know that we are able to listen at His gates so we can advance.

As we give Him our best, God will see to it that we are fully compensated for all our troubles and bring relief. So, let's start to acknowledge His rule and bring Him all our concerns and cares. It takes a concerted effort to stay focused on Jesus, but as we determine to stay on fire for Him, He is able to bring us to a place of restoration.

There is no such thing as the "microwave style" of Christianity. We must marinate in His presence, until we enter into God's glory. He is pleased when we allow Him full access to our hearts. It is the heart condition that determines our proximity to God. The process of being hidden allows us to be conformed to the Lord's image, and to know Him in the fellowship of His sufferings. We are then enabled to be molded and shaped by the Master's hand into a vessel of honor. Then we are truly able to be the city on a hill which cannot be hidden.

PATIENCE IN THE PROCESS

GOD'S TIMING IS PERFECT

There is a time to be lifted up because promotion comes from the Lord. But what a leader learns is that it's "'Not by might nor by power, but by My Spirit,' says the Lord of hosts" (Zechariah 4:6). When the flesh is dead, the Lord is able to redeem what was thought to be lost. It is time for the servant of God to remain faithful and to continue to do the work assigned to him. As we labor in private, God will bring us into public in due time.

It reminds me of the story of Esther, and how one night the king could not sleep and how he opened the books where it was recorded that Mordecai saved his life. He was rewarded with a royal robe, and he was lead on horse through the streets, proclaiming before Mordecai, "Thus shall it be done to the man whom the king delights to honor!" (Esther 6:9). This is how it will be for us. We will be honored for our ability to persevere and not lose heart. Hebrews 10:35-36 states, "Therefore do not cast away your confidence, which has great reward. For you have need of endurance, so that after you have done the will of God, you may receive the promise." Mordecai's blessing happened suddenly.

"Suddenlies" do happen and the good things you do won't go unnoticed by God. He is keeping His record books, and pay day is coming. What you have done in secret, God will reward you openly. He is bringing many into places of authority. What He has allowed for evil can and will be taken back and there will be a day of recompense. Forgiveness is essential to progress.

Consider Job, a righteous man who endured much affliction and suffered the loss of his children. He kept the faith, even though friends told him it was his fault. In the end, the Lord blessed him when he forgave.

Job 42:10 says, "And the LORD restored Job's losses when he prayed for his friends. Indeed the LORD gave Job twice as much as he had before."

Because he endured the test, Job was rewarded with a visitation of glory. God pulled back the curtain and revealed himself to Job in a whirlwind. Not only did Job see God, he also heard God's voice as God revealed Himself powerfully to Job's heart through wisdom and revelation. Job received a thrilling encounter with God because he persevered.[2]

Many of God's saints have had to endure the wait and trying circumstances, but the glory of God's visitation made it all worthwhile. The expected end keeps us turning the pages of our storybook. All our hard work and acts of service will pay off. Waiting in faith, will cause God's goodness to come to pass in your life. Those who withstand the tests and keep the faith are candidates for God's glory. Again, it boils down to faith and patience. We must not shrink back and harden our hearts. It's the perseverance of the saints that will outlast the enemy!

Moses was called of God to lead the Israelites out of Egypt. The call of God on his life came at a time when he knew he could not rely on himself anymore. Moses knew it would take more than a mere man to deliver the Israelites. Moses accepted the call, because he knew God would be with him.

2. Bob Sorge, Glory When Heaven Invades Earth, Greenwood, Missouri Oasis House, 2000.

The Purpose of Being Hidden

A holy desperation keeps us crying out for more. We must ask for a hunger to see Him in all of His glory. For just as there are levels of God's presence, so there are levels of God's glory. Moses not only encountered God in the burning bush, but when he asked for His glory, God showed him his back. His training in the wilderness, had served him well. Moses became a humble servant of great stature.

FILLED WITH THE SPIRIT

We must stay filled with the Spirit so we are able to see Jesus in all fullness. It takes a seeing heart to comprehend spiritual truth. The Holy Spirit allows us to discern what is revealed to our inner man. This enables us to remain steadfast during trials.

Paul writes during his imprisonment in Rome to the churches in Ephesians 1:17-18, "[For I always pray to] the God of our Lord Jesus Christ, the Father of glory, that He may grant you a spirit of wisdom and revelation [of insight into mysteries and secrets] in the [deep and intimate] knowledge of Him, by having the eyes of your heart flooded with light, so that you can know and understand the hope to which He has called you, and how rich is His glorious inheritance in the saints (His set-apart ones)" (AMP).

These are excellent verses to pray, as they show what is needed to withstand the onslaught of the enemy. We must keep the vision fresh of what the Lord is saying not only to the churches, but to us today. We need a word of encouragement from the Lord that will enable us to do battle with. As we grow weary, we need to be refreshed by God's Spirit working in our lives. We cannot go by yesterday's word; we need fresh manna from the throne room so we can know what God is doing in our lives this very moment. "And Jesus replied to him, It is written, Man shall not live and be sustained by (on) bread alone but by every word and expression of God" (Luke 4:4, AMP).

STAY FOCUSED

As we keep our wits about us, we are enabled to show others that we really believe God is working to bring us to a place of safety. We are being read by others, so what we believe can be seen to all at this time. We are not abandoned by the Lord; we are entering into a place of healing as we keep our minds focused on the Lord's plan and purpose for our lives.

A few years back I had a vision of the Lord where He was behind an old fashioned camera. It was the one with the cover over the camera, and you cannot see the person taking the picture. I was looking around, to and fro, and the Lord said, "Look to me, look to me." When He said this I looked straight ahead, into the camera. We must keep our eyes focused on Him. We cannot give in to our feelings; we must be convinced that He is greater than our fears. Hebrews 12:2 reiterates this by saying, "Looking away [from all that will distract] to Jesus, Who is the Leader and the Source of our faith [giving the first incentive for our belief] and is also its Finisher [bringing it to maturity and perfection]. He, for the joy [of obtaining the prize] that was set before Him, endured the cross, despising and ignoring the shame, and is now seated at the right hand of the throne of God" (AMP). Jesus kept His focus by praying to the Father and keeping an eternal perspective. He did not allow the pain of the moment to distract Him from fulfilling His purpose.

God is able to bring healing and restoration into your life. He wants you to remain at peace through the storms. We must remain stable in the storms so we can pray.

The Purpose of Being Hidden

When the heavens seem like brass, we can rely on God's promises and what He has spoken to us to give us hope. We must stop relying on what we see going on in the natural. A carnal man relies on his own understanding of events, but a man whom God commends, relies on the Spirit to gain discernment. As we live by our spirit we are enabled to bear up under the pressure of false accusations, and loss. We are being taken to a place where we can no longer rely on our own insight, we must seek the Lord.

One of the dangers during the hidden season is to do things in our own strength. By relying on our own experience we can miss God. We must seek His face so we can know what honors the Lord. We must keep in mind that He wants us to rely on Him for our sustenance and not allow man to take the glory that's truly God's. He is teaching us how to move in sync with the Holy Spirit. We are being given the roadmap from which to travel.

Even in church services, we need to welcome the Holy Spirit. We have to come to a place where we drop any preconceived ideas about how to please God and consult Him to give us His agenda. When we give Jesus the freedom to move in our services, He comes on the scene and makes His presence known. He wants to fill our temple with His glory. The glory that was present from the beginning of time. But it takes a heart that is fully consecrated to Him, willing to seek His face above all else. As His people begin to consecrate themselves and give up what is harmful, then they will begin to see an increase in anointing and power. It's not what you think He wants from you, but what you allow Him to change that will bring Him glory.

It's not always about getting out of a bad situation, but allowing God's grace to change you before He will adjust your circumstances. We have to know that He is aware of the situation, before you even know what you need to do. We have to allow His rod of correction to have its way in our lives. As we allow Jesus to take what He wants out of our lives, then we are enabled to be a vessel of honor that is fully pleasing to Him. He waits in anticipation for the saints to reach full stature.

ENJOY THE PROCESS

We cannot rush what God is doing in us. If we allow discouragement to take hold, we can grow distant from the Lord and revert to doing things our own way. When a person loses sensitivity to the Lord they set themselves up for deception. By submitting to the testing process, we will later share in His glory.

As we gain wisdom in the hidden seasons of our lives, we are able to be fire carriers, bearing the torch for the Lord. We become His mouthpiece as we allow ourselves to be sculpted and shaped according to His exact specifications. As we allow testing to conform our lives, we become a flame that will spread the glory of God and in the process become a weapon of warfare. We become strong in the Lord and the power of His might (Ephesians 6:10).

We are developing God's character when we allow Him to take what we think will bring us happiness in favor of losing our lives. In relinquishment, we learn to submit to His timing and purpose.

By believing that the Lord is faithful to fulfill His call on our lives, we are able to trust His promises and declare His goodness. 1 Thessalonians 5:24 says, "Faithful is He Who is calling you [to Himself] and utterly trustworthy, and He will also do it [fulfill His call by hallowing and keeping you]" (AMP).

The Purpose of Being Hidden

Hallowing, according to the Webster's dictionary, means to "make holy, sanctify and consecrate."[3] God is making us ready. We need an enlarged vision to see what the Lord is doing in our lives. By keeping our vision alive, we stay encouraged during the times of doubt. We are not alone in our struggles, but we are being prepared to step into our season of fulfillment.

---

3. Webster's Dictionary, s.v. "Hallowing." (Accessed 7-8-2011).

ABOUT THE AUTHOR

Rhoda Banks, LCSW is a Messanic Jew who came to the Lord after a series of prophetic dreams, where she saw Jesus on the cross who told her to believe in Him.

Shortly afterwards she attended Columbia University in New York, where she graduated with a Master's Degree in Social Work. While working in the field, she began to understand the importance of faith-based values. As a result she attended Alliance Theological Seminary before entering private practice in 1998.

Rhoda has a teaching and preaching gift. She is the founder of Restoration Ministries, a ministry designed to encourage, mature and heal the broken- hearted, in response to the Lord's call. She desires to see the body of Christ come into the fullness for which Christ died. She is a respected prophetic voice in the body of Christ.

Rhoda has been a keynote speaker at Women's Aglow Conferences and other Seminars throughout the Northeast. She enjoys speaking on worship and has served on the Worship Team at International Worship Center and other churches.

Rhoda has been in private practice for the past twenty five years. During this time, she has ministered to the lost and has seen many lives transformed by the power of Christ. Her counseling background provides her a unique platform of instructing the Body of Christ, as well as inspiring them to walk in sound biblical principles.

She is the author of *Favor: The Ingredient for Success, The Purpose of Being Hidden,* and *Dance as David Danced: The Return of Davidic Worship. Davidic Worship: Strategies for Breakthrough in the End Times* is the updated, second edition of this published work. For further information, visit rhodabanks.com.

Other Books by Rhoda Banks

Favor: The Ingredient for Success by Rhoda Banks

Favor: The Ingredient for Success by Rhoda Banks is a concise guide to the factors that cause one to advance.

Through biblical principles found in Scripture, the author clearly describes the importance of the favor of God and how to obtain it.

Dance as David Danced by Rhoda Banks

Dance as David Danced: The Return of Davidic Worship by Rhoda Banks reveals how intimacy with God develops through worship.

The church will see a shift in the spiritual climate as praise leads the way to overturn the enemy's plans.